"As a marriage and family therapist, I wholeheartedly recommend this transformative journal for liberating yourself from people-pleasing, codependency, and unhealthy relationship patterns. Setting itself apart, this unique journal features straightforward checklists and empowering prompts to guide you in establishing and communicating boundaries effectively. Essential for overcoming fear, fostering self-awareness, and embracing your authenticity, it serves as a practical and invaluable guide on your healing journey!"

—**Kristen D. Boice, LMFT**, owner of Pathways to Healing Counseling, and host of the *Close the Chapter* podcast

"Sharon Martin takes you on a journey to discover and understand your boundaries through this journal. It explores all aspects of boundaries from myths to your motivation to change. It helps one discover what stands in the way of establishing and following through on boundary setting, and how to move past that. This journal is a useful tool that will give you the skills to create important and lasting change."

—**Jessica Fowler, LCSW**, host of the *What Your Therapist Is Reading* podcast

"Sharon Martin's new book, *The Better Boundaries Guided Journal*, is a wonderful resource! The journal explores all the ways we might get stuck creating and holding boundaries, and provides thoughtful, compassionate prompts to work through those obstacles. I highly recommend Martin's journal to anyone who needs support and guidance with boundary setting."

—**Elizabeth Cush, LCPC**, licensed clinical professional counselor, life coach for highly sensitive women, and host of the *Awaken Your Wise Woman* podcast

T0299673

"If you struggle with how to set healthy boundaries or think you can't, this guided journal is a must! Sharon assists you in exploring your beliefs on boundaries, how to create them, and ways to practice your new skills. It can transform your life from over-whelmed and stressed out to empowered and fulfilled. I highly recommend this journal to my clients."

—**Nicole Burgess, LMFT**, host of the *Launching Your Daughter* and *Soulfilled Sisterhood* podcasts

"This journal feels like a highly skilled therapist holding your hand, step by step, through the personal process of changing your daily lived experience. Sharon provides a safe space to not just talk about the need for boundaries, but to do something about them and adjust behaviors over time. Her warmth and care radiate off of the pages!"

—**Caitlin Faas, PhD**, author of *Unstuck*

"*The Better Boundaries Guided Journal* guided me step by step through how to identify and set my boundaries. This journal made me feel encouraged and supported while showing me how to improve my boundaries. Sharon's journal is a much-needed resource for how to move past old beliefs that no longer serve me. This is truly an amazing resource for anyone wanting to learn about setting boundaries and moving past the fears that often accompany them."

—**Michelle Farris**, psychotherapist, codependency expert, avid growth seeker, and author of *The Self-Trust Journal* and *The Codependency Workbook*

"In circumstances where boundaries are blurred or unestablished, Sharon Martin brings the opportunity to gain insight and clarity with *The Better Boundaries Guided Journal*. Using a well-considered process, it is possible for the reader to navigate the complex landscape of relationships, self-care, and personal growth. With each page, Sharon Martin empowers readers to honor their self-journey, while cultivating the possibility for fulfilling connections. Recommended for anyone on the path to establishing their sense of self in the midst of a relationship."

—**Hope Eden, LCSW**, founder of The Organized Therapist

New Harbinger Journals for Change

Research shows that journaling has a universally positive effect on mental health. But in the midst of life's difficulties—such as stress, anxiety, depression, relationship problems, parenting challenges, or even obsessive or negative thoughts—where do you begin? New Harbinger *Journals for Change* combine evidence-based psychology with proven-effective guided journaling techniques to help you make lasting personal change—one page at a time. Written by renowned mental health and wellness experts, *Journals for Change* provide a creative and safe space to process difficult emotions, work through challenges, reflect on what matters, and set intentions for the future.

Since 1973, New Harbinger has published practical, user-friendly self-help books and workbooks to help readers make positive change. Our *Journals for Change* offer the same powerfully effective tools—without ever *feeling* like therapy. If you're committed to improving your mental health, these easy-to-use guided journals can help you take small, actionable steps toward lasting well-being.

For a complete list of journals in our *Journals for Change* series, visit newharbinger.com.

THE
BETTER
BOUNDARIES
Guided Journal

A SAFE SPACE TO REFLECT ON YOUR NEEDS *and*

WORK TOWARD HEALTHY, RESPECTFUL RELATIONSHIPS

SHARON MARTIN, DSW, LCSW

New Harbinger Publications, Inc.

Publisher's Note

This publication is designed to provide accurate and authoritative information in regard to the subject matter covered. It is sold with the understanding that the publisher is not engaged in rendering psychological, financial, legal, or other professional services. If expert assistance or counseling is needed, the services of a competent professional should be sought.

NEW HARBINGER PUBLICATIONS is a registered trademark of New Harbinger Publications, Inc.

New Harbinger Publications is an employee-owned company.

Copyright © 2024 by Sharon Martin
New Harbinger Publications, Inc.
5720 Shattuck Avenue
Oakland, CA 94609
www.newharbinger.com

All Rights Reserved

Cover design by Amy Daniel

Interior design by Amy Shoup

Acquired by Ryan Buresh

NCEO
MEMBER

FSC
www.fsc.org
MIX
Paper | Supporting
responsible forestry
FSC® C008955

Printed in the United States of America

26   25   24

10   9   8   7   6   5   4   3   2   1   First Printing

Contents

PART 3:
Set Better Boundaries

PART 4:
Practice Healthy Communication

PART 5:
Keep Learning

Introduction

You probably picked up this journal because you feel depleted and discouraged. Maybe it's been hard to find time for yourself because you put everyone else's needs before your own. Perhaps you find it hard to say no—or you feel guilty when you do. Or maybe you feel resentful because others just don't seem to understand your needs, and you don't know how to get them to respect you and the boundaries you set. If so, you're in the right place. That's what this journal is all about!

At the center of this journey to setting boundaries is the question: What would it look like to put yourself first?

It can be a tough question to answer, especially if you're used to people-pleasing and self-sacrificing behavior. This journal is an important first step. What's great about journaling—beyond all the evidence of how beneficial and therapeutic it can be—is that when you give yourself space to explore *how you feel* and *what you need*, changing your life becomes possible. Journaling is a way to understand yourself and build confidence in your abilities. I hope this journal will be a safe space for you to do the work necessary to understand your needs and articulate them with confidence—to set the boundaries you need to set and *keep* them.

In this journal, you'll be guided to consider your feelings around setting boundaries and what it might look like if you saw this as an act of kindness to yourself and others rather than something cruel. You'll learn how you can journal your way through ambivalence, guilt, fear of selfishness, and other barriers that often get in our way. These feelings are totally normal to have, but they can hijack you and keep you stuck in patterns that don't work for you.

You'll also examine all manner of relationships in your life. It's common for people to come to a journal like this with one relationship in mind. But the truth is, as social creatures, we're often pushed and pulled in many directions at once because of all the demands on our time. So, this journal is designed for you to reflect on lots of areas—work, family, friends, and more—where setting healthy and effective boundaries can benefit you. If you feel that you already have solid boundaries in a particular area, feel free to skip that section.

You'll also learn effective boundary-setting skills and consider how best to handle boundary violations. Boundaries are crucial when dealing with toxic and difficult people, so we'll touch on this as well. Keep in mind, though, that depending on the severity of someone's toxicity, this journal may not be enough. If you're in a violent or threatening relationship, please seek help from a mental health professional, law enforcement, a crisis line, a family violence organization, or another professional.

Lastly, you'll work on setting and maintaining boundaries with yourself so you can create healthy habits and feel in control of your life. You'll also practice healthy communication skills. These will help you successfully communicate your needs and limits to others while remaining calm and confident during difficult conversations.

You picked this journal to be guided through the process of finally communicating and getting what you need from the relationships in your life. Take a deep breath because the journey starts now!

Why You Need Boundaries

Why do you want to learn how to set boundaries? Use this checklist to identify the ways in which your life is affected by a lack of consistent boundaries.

- ○ I'm afraid to say no and don't want to disappoint people.

- ○ I don't speak up when I want something or when I'm mistreated.

- ○ I frequently feel angry, resentful, or overwhelmed.

- ○ I don't communicate my expectations to others.

- ○ I feel physically or emotionally unsafe.

- ○ I don't make time for self-care.

- ○ I feel guilty when I set limits or do things for myself.

- ○ I make commitments that I later regret.

- ○ I am frequently overscheduled, rushed, or tired.

- ○ I do things out of obligation rather than personal choice.

- ○ I don't spend enough quality time with the people I care about.

- ○ I don't have a strong sense of who I am, my values, interests, and goals.

- ○ I am tuned into how other people feel but don't always know how I feel.

- ○ I accept blame for things I didn't do or couldn't control.
- ○ I enable others to be irresponsible by doing things for them that they could do themselves.
- ○ I feel obligated to answer personal questions.
- ○ I loan money or possessions to people who don't return them.
- ○ People take advantage of me.
- ○ My children don't respect my limits and walk all over me.
- ○ My children act entitled or spoiled.
- ○ I feel burned-out at work.
- ○ I spend a lot of time, energy, or money trying to fix or solve other people's problems.
- ○ I act passive-aggressively instead of directly expressing my feelings and needs.
- ○ I think I don't matter or am not as important as others.
- ○ I overshare personal information or get close to people before trust is established.
- ○ I blame others for things I'm responsible for.
- ○ I harm others by not respecting their privacy, possessions, feelings, or bodies.
- ○ I struggle with self-discipline, such as managing my money, time, eating, or social media use.

How else has not having boundaries negatively affected you? Be as specific as possible.

_____

_____

_____

_____

_____

_____

How do you define boundaries? What purpose do they serve?

_____

_____

_____

_____

_____

_____

_____

_____

> Boundaries create a healthy separation between you and others and define who you are, so you can be yourself and make choices that are right for you.

How do you think boundaries will improve your life?

_____

_____

_____

_____

_____

_____

How will boundaries improve your relationships with others?

_____

_____

_____

_____

Boundaries can be
a self-management
tool that helps us
prioritize healthy
habits like getting
enough sleep,
minimizing alcohol
intake, and exercising.

_____

_____

_____

_____

_____

_____

How will boundaries improve your emotional and physical health?

_____

_____

_____

_____

_____

_____

_____

How will boundaries improve your self-esteem or relationship with yourself?

_____

_____

_____

_____

_____

_____

_____

_____

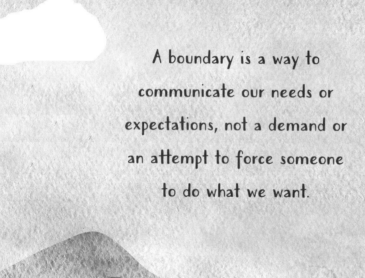

A boundary is a way to communicate our needs or expectations, not a demand or an attempt to force someone to do what we want.

PART I

Overcome Barriers to Setting Boundaries

Even when you see the benefits of boundaries, it's normal to feel apprehensive about making a significant change.

What concerns do you have about setting boundaries? What has held you back from setting boundaries in the past?

_____

_____

_____

_____

_____

_____

_____

_____

_____

_____

_____

_____

Boundary Myths

One of the big reasons we avoid setting boundaries is that we mistakenly think they're mean and will lead to conflict and disconnection. However, boundaries are inherently respectful because they communicate our expectations and help others understand how to interact with us—what's okay and what's not okay. Boundaries are a way to meet your needs, not a way to punish or control others.

Have you experienced setting or receiving boundaries as mean or hurtful? If so, what do you think made the experience feel this way?

_____

_____

_____

_____

Can you imagine setting or receiving boundaries as an act of kindness? What would that sound like, or what would the situation be?

_____

_____

_____

_____

What would make the difference between a boundary feeling hurtful and feeling kind?

_____

_____

_____

_____

_____

Another common misconception about boundaries is that they're selfish. However, just because they're for your well-being, doesn't mean they're selfish.

Think of a time when the fear of being selfish kept you from setting boundaries. Did you feel compelled to accommodate the other person's needs or put your own preferences to one side, even as part of you wished not to? Describe what happened.

_____

_____

_____

_____

_____

_____

In the situation you described, what would be the middle ground between selfish and selfless? How would it feel to choose that middle ground?

_____

_____

_____

_____

_____

_____

If it's hard to stop thinking of boundaries as selfish, you can use affirmations to reinforce a new way of thinking. Circle one of the examples below that works as an affirmation for you.

"It's healthy, not selfish, for me to
[maintain my exercise routine/say no to things/set limits]."

• • •

"It's okay to prioritize my own needs."

• • •

"I'm not responsible for my
[father's/partner's/friend's/whoever's] feelings."

• • •

"Sometimes being honest is the best form of kindness."

Or you can try writing your own affirmations for the times you struggle to be assertive.

_____

_____

_____

_____

_____

You can also think about how setting boundaries will serve both you and those around you in the long run. How will setting boundaries and prioritizing your self-care have a positive impact on your loved ones or colleagues?

_____

_____

_____

Learning to set boundaries isn't about convincing or forcing others to do what you want; boundaries are about expressing yourself clearly and asking for what you need.

_____

_____

_____

_____

Finding the Right Balance

Boundaries need to be strong but not rigid. If we create boundaries that are rigid, we risk isolating ourselves. In contrast, if we have boundaries that are weak, we'll be left vulnerable and unprotected. Ultimately, we need boundaries that flex to accommodate different situations, different relationships, and our changing needs.

Consider your boundaries right now. Do you tend to have boundaries that are too rigid, too weak, or a combination?

_____

What kinds of problems have boundaries that are too rigid or too weak caused you?

_____

_____

_____

_____

_____

_____

_____

Identify two or three situations where it would be helpful for you to have flexible boundaries or times when you've adapted your boundaries to make them healthy.

_____

_____

_____

_____

_____

_____

Below is a list of phrases that describe boundaries. These phrases can help you challenge any negative associations you may have about boundaries and remind you that boundaries are both good and necessary. Circle the phrases that can help you see boundaries in a positive light and add any others that you can think of.

Boundaries are:

- well thought-out, clear, and direct.

- statements or actions that express what you need or want.

- limits that protect your health, safety, and resources.

- kind.

- a form of self-care.

- choices that help you feel safe.

- part of every healthy relationship.

- _____

- _____

Which was your favorite phrase?

_____

_____

We all know that setting boundaries is hard, but have you ever wondered why? What makes setting boundaries hard for you?

_____

_____

_____

_____

_____

_____

_____

Understanding what makes it hard for you to set boundaries will help you change the thoughts and behaviors that get in the way of setting healthy boundaries.

The Influence of Your Family of Origin

We learn a lot about setting boundaries by watching others—our parents, friends, coworkers, and even fictional characters in books and movies. Our parents or caretakers usually have the greatest influence on us and our boundaries—especially when we're young and most impressionable—because we spend considerable time with them.

Who modeled healthy boundaries for you? (If you can't think of anyone that you know in person, there might be a character from a book or show.) Describe what these boundaries were like.

_____

_____

_____

_____

Who modeled unhealthy boundaries for you? Meaning, boundaries that were too weak or too rigid and got in the way of relationships rather than serving them? Describe what these boundaries were like.

_____

_____

_____

_____

Did the family you grew up in have rigid boundaries, weak boundaries, or a mix of both? Were boundaries and limits consistent or inconsistent, flexible or inflexible, clear or confusing? What was that like for you as a child?

_____

_____

_____

_____

_____

_____

How have the boundary problems in your childhood family made it difficult for you to set boundaries now? Did they impact your communication style, self-esteem, sense of safety, or ability to trust?

_____

_____

_____

_____

_____

_____

If your family didn't model healthy boundaries or teach you about them, don't be discouraged. Setting boundaries is a skill that everyone can learn, no matter their age.

Challenge Your Fears

Asserting your individuality, asking for what you need, and setting boundaries can be scary because either you've tried and gotten poor results or setting boundaries is a new skill and you're not sure how to do it or what the outcome will be.

Which of these fears about setting boundaries do you identify with?

- ○ Hurting someone's feelings
- ○ Conflict or anger
- ○ Suffering physical abuse
- ○ Being ignored
- ○ Being misunderstood
- ○ Being criticized, ridiculed, or not taken seriously
- ○ Disappointing or displeasing someone
- ○ Losing a relationship (rejection or abandonment)
- ○ Giving in or not being able to maintain your boundaries
- ○ Being unworthy of respect
- ○ Realizing your loved one doesn't care about you

As you reflect on these fears, what stands out to you?

_____

_____

_____

_____

_____

_____

_____

Fears are often based on misperceptions or what psychologists call *cognitive distortions*. Or they may result from past experiences. But even these fears are often overgeneralized. If fear has been impeding your ability to set boundaries, use the exercise that follows to challenge your fear-based beliefs and determine whether they're accurate.

Identify your fear. If I set boundaries, _____

_____

Example: *If I set boundaries, everyone will hate me.*

Identify the underlying belief. I believe _____

_____

Example: *I believe I'm difficult and people don't like me.*

What evidence is there for or against what you believe?

_____

_____

_____

_____

_____

Example: It's true Paul got angry when I told him I wasn't going to his parents' with him. But I stand up for myself at work, and they seem to respect me. And I get along with my roommate, so not everyone finds me difficult.

Looking at the evidence against your belief, try to rewrite your fear as a more accurate and supportive statement.

_____

_____

_____

_____

_____

Example: Some people may get angry when I set boundaries with them. But some people do respect my boundaries. Setting boundaries doesn't make me difficult.

Let Go of Guilt

Guilt is the feeling you have when you think you've done something wrong. When you feel guilty about setting boundaries, it's often because you think you don't have the right to protect yourself, say no, have your own ideas, or ask for something.

Which of these beliefs contribute to your guilt about setting boundaries?

- ○ I shouldn't need or want anything.

- ○ If I do need or want something, I shouldn't ask for it.

- ○ It's my responsibility to take care of others.

- ○ Being selfless is a virtue.

- ○ I should always put others before myself.

- ○ I should keep my opinions to myself. No one wants to hear them.

- ○ What I want doesn't matter.

- ○ It's mean, rude, or wrong to say no.

- ○ It's selfish to consider my own needs.

These beliefs are all based on an inequitable relationship where another person's rights and needs are assumed to be more important than yours.

Boundaries are built on the idea that we all have the same rights and that you matter as much as everyone else.

Have you ever thought that you don't have the right to set boundaries? That you don't deserve to be treated with respect? Or that you're not worth the effort? If so, where do you think these beliefs came from?

_____

_____

_____

_____

_____

_____

_____

_____

_____

_____

Below are some examples of personal rights. Check off the ones that resonate with you. Add others too! Make this list as specific as possible to make it useful to you.

○ I have the right to be treated with respect and kindness.

○ I have the right to say no.

○ I have the right to change my mind.

○ I have the right to be physically and emotionally safe.

○ I have the right to my own thoughts, feelings, values, and beliefs.

○ I have the right to happiness and pleasure.

○ I have the right to rest.

○ I have the right to privacy.

○ I have the right to share or not share my possessions.

○ I have the right to decide what's best for me.

○ I have the right to distance myself from or end relationships with negative or hurtful people.

○ I have the right to pursue my goals.

○ I have the right to set boundaries.

○ I have the right to _____

○ I have the right to _____

○ I have the right to _____

Are any of these personal rights difficult for you to accept? Why do you think that is?

_____

_____

_____

_____

If a friend told you that they didn't think they had the right to _____

(fill in the blank with any of the personal rights that you struggle with),

what would you say to them?

_____

_____

_____

Now, try telling yourself the same thing to reinforce that these personal rights apply to you too.

Rewrite what you'd say to a friend so you can practice saying it to yourself.

_____

_____

_____

_____

To continue building confidence in your personal rights, examine what your personal rights look like in your life.

Identify a personal right: _____

What does this personal right look like in your daily life?

_____

_____

_____

_____

_____

Another way to recognize your inherent worth is to treat yourself with respect and kindness. To put this into practice, deliberately do three acts of self-care every day. They don't need to be glamorous or time-consuming, but they do need to be meaningful and intentional.

What three self-care activities will you do today?

1. _____

2. _____

3. _____

For maximum benefit, record your three self-care activities daily and, as you do them, say to yourself, *I'm doing this because I matter.*

Day One

1. _____

2. _____

3. _____

Day Two

1. _____

2. _____

3. _____

Day Three

1. _____

2. _____

3. _____

Know Yourself and What You Need

Your boundaries are unique to you. So it's hard to set boundaries if you don't have a clear sense of who you are and what you need. For example, if you don't know what you need or want, you can't ask for it or meet the need yourself. And if you don't know what matters to you or what your goals are, you can't set boundaries to protect them.

Building self-understanding is an ongoing process. It's not something you can accomplish in a week or a month. But answering the following questions is a way to start the process.

What are you good at? _____

_____

_____

What are your short-term goals? And long-term goals? _____

_____

_____

Who matters most to you? _____

_____

_____

_____

Who can you go to for support or help? _____

_____

_____

What do you like to do for fun? _____

_____

_____

What do you value? What do you believe in? _____

_____

_____

Where or when do you feel safest? _____

_____

_____

What or who gives you comfort? _____

_____

_____

_____

_____

_____

What are you passionate about? _____

_____

_____

_____

What are you grateful for? _____

_____

_____

_____

_____

How do you learn best (doing, watching, listening, reading)? _____

_____

_____

How do you know that you're feeling stressed or upset? _____

_____

_____

What makes you feel respected? _____

_____

_____

_____

What makes you feel loved? _____

_____

_____

_____

What makes you feel safe? _____

_____

_____

Another strategy for getting to know yourself is to keep a record of your likes and dislikes. This is a simple way to learn more about your preferences, personality, and needs, which will later help you identify boundaries that will increase your life satisfaction.

Date: _____

Things I liked today:

1. _____

2. _____

3. _____

Things I didn't like today:

1. _____

2. _____

3. _____

Is there anything I wish had been different for me today?

_____

_____

_____

_____

_____

_____

Date: _____

Things I liked today:

1. _____

2. _____

3. _____

Things I didn't like today:

1. _____

2. _____

3. _____

Is there anything I wish had been different for me today?

_____

_____

_____

_____

_____

Date: _____

Things I liked today:

1. _____

2. _____

3. _____

Things I didn't like today:

1. _____

2. _____

3. _____

Is there anything I wish had been different for me today?

_____

_____

_____

_____

_____

_____

Date: _____

Things I liked today:

   1. _____

   2. _____

   3. _____

Things I didn't like today:

   1. _____

   2. _____

   3. _____

Is there anything I wish had been different for me today?

_____

_____

_____

_____

_____

Your boundaries tell your boss, coworkers, friends, family, and others how they can treat you or what you're willing to do.

PART 2

Assess Your

Relationships

This section is divided into common relationship domains: work relationships, intimate partners, children, extended family and friends, and difficult people. It starts with work because these relationships are often simpler and have explicit channels of communication. As we continue, we'll address more complex and interdependent relationships.

Boundaries at Work

Take a few moments to think about your current work situation. (If you're not currently doing paid work, you can refer to volunteer work or a previous job.)

What boundary issues have you experienced? How did they affect your job performance, job satisfaction, and personal life?

_____

_____

_____

_____

_____

With your personal rights in mind, what boundaries do you need to set?

_____

_____

_____

_____

_____

Often, we don't have as many choices or as much power at work as we do in our personal lives. As a result, you may have limited options for resolving boundary issues.

If the other people involved aren't willing or able to change, is there a way for you to make changes that will meet your needs at work? And if not, what other options do you see?

When you've identified options for handling your boundary problems, whether they're actions you take with others or on your own, notice whether you feel any resistance or judgment toward them. Explore your feelings. Be curious about what this resistance or judgment is about, and see if you can find a more positive way to look at your options.

What underlies this resistance or judgment?

What are the potential positive outcomes?

_____

_____

_____

_____

_____

If you don't have the power to resolve your boundary issues, you may need to ask for help from a supervisor, administrator, attorney, union representative, or someone else.

What kind of help do you need? Who might you ask?

_____

_____

_____

_____

What feels difficult, stressful, or scary about asking for help?

_____

_____

_____

_____

_____

There's no guarantee, of course, that seeking help will get you the result that you want. When we make decisions, we're always weighing the potential benefits against the potential drawbacks. And when we're talking about our jobs, paychecks, and professional standing, we need to consider our options carefully. With that in mind, what do you see as the potential benefits and risks of seeking help? How likely are you to achieve your desired outcome with or without help?

What might you gain by setting boundaries at work, even if they aren't entirely successful? What would attempting to set boundaries and being assertive say about you? Alternatively, what would being passive tell your colleagues and employer?

Boundaries with Your Partner

Think about your intimate relationships. Have boundary issues contributed to problems with your current or past partners? How?

_____

_____

_____

_____

Boundaries are the agreements that govern our relationships. They tell our partners how we want to be treated—which behaviors are permissible and which aren't. Abiding by these agreements or boundaries creates the emotional and physical safety we all need to build intimacy and trust. They also reduce conflict, blame, and resentment because they delineate who's responsible for what in a partnership.

How do you hope boundaries will improve your relationship with your partner (or future partners)?

_____

_____

_____

_____

_____

Now, think about the agreements you have with your partner (or have had with past partners).

_____

_____

_____

_____

Which agreements work well?

_____

_____

_____

_____

Which areas cause conflict because one or both of you violate the agreements (or perhaps no agreements were ever made)?

_____

_____

_____

_____

Use the space below to identify the boundary issue you most want to work on with your partner.

_____

_____

_____

Most boundary conflicts can be resolved through compromise if you're both willing to give a bit and are interested in each other's needs and feelings. Use the questions that follow to practice.

What do you need in this situation?

_____

_____

_____

_____

What does your partner need? (It's best to ask rather than assume.)

_____

_____

_____

_____

> Healthy boundaries can help you create the right amount of connection and separateness in your relationship, so you have the trust and intimacy that you desire while also maintaining your individuality.

What are some ways for you and your partner to compromise, so you both get your needs met sufficiently?

_____

_____

_____

_____

Sometimes, we feel so strongly about an issue, such as fidelity or child-rearing, that it's hard to compromise. What boundary issues with your partner do you feel strongly about or place a high value on?

_____

_____

_____

_____

What issues do you think your partner feels strongly about or places a high value on?

_____

_____

_____

_____

Being aware of your and your partner's "hot-button" issues can help you approach compromise with more empathy and openness to change. If you're having trouble compromising, the following questions can help you.

Why do I feel so strongly about this? Is there a way for me to flex a little without giving up an important value or need?

_____

_____

_____

_____

_____

_____

_____

_____

Ultimately, compromise takes empathy, the ability to understand your partner's feelings and needs, and the ability to delay gratification or go without. It's also a skill most people can learn with practice and help from a relationship therapist if needed.

Boundaries with Your Children

If you have children, think about the limits or boundaries you have with them and why you set those boundaries. When we set boundaries with our children, we're teaching them about responsibility, assertiveness, self-management, and other skills they need to be physically and emotionally healthy.

What are your boundary battles with your children? When do they happen? Who's involved?

_____

_____

_____

_____

_____

What do you hope to gain by setting better boundaries with your children? How will your life improve?

_____

_____

_____

_____

What do you hope your children will learn or gain when you set boundaries with them?

_____

_____

_____

_____

_____

_____

Setting boundaries with your children is hard work, and there are numerous ways we can get tripped up. Which of these common boundary-setting errors do you struggle with?

○ I overestimate what my child is developmentally capable of and have unrealistic rules and expectations.

○ I don't enforce boundaries consistently.

○ I have too many rules, which confuse my children, and I spend precious time and energy enforcing rules that aren't that important.

○ The consequences aren't related to the problem behavior.

○ I lose my cool and overreact.

The boundaries that you set for your children need to align with their abilities and change as they mature.

With your child's social, emotional, and cognitive abilities in mind, do you think any of your rules or expectations are unrealistic? If so, which ones? How might you make them more developmentally appropriate?

_____

_____

_____

_____

Do you have any questions about what you can reasonably expect your child to do? Note those that you'd like to research further or discuss with a professional, such as your child's pediatrician.

_____

_____

_____

_____

_____

We're all inconsistent with our boundaries at times, and we shouldn't expect perfection from ourselves. However, we can strive to communicate clearly with our children and to stay true to our word more often than not. Let's start by assessing your consistency with boundaries as a parent. Then you'll identify steps you can take to be more consistent.

What gets in the way of you being consistent? Use a 0–10 scale to rate each option.

_____ Being tired or overwhelmed

_____ Disagreeing with my partner or other caregiver about rules and consequences

_____ Feeling anger

_____ Feeling guilt

_____ Feeling fear

_____ Wanting my children to like me

_____ Not knowing what appropriate boundaries and consequences are

_____ Other: _____

For the items you rated with a 5 or higher, what would help you address these barriers? For example, if anger is a barrier for you, would you benefit from taking an anger management class, getting more sleep, or meditating? If you feel stuck, try to identify _why_ you're experiencing these obstacles.

_____

_____

_____

_____

_____

What specific actions can you take to overcome these obstacles and be more consistent? For instance, if you think an anger management class would be helpful, you might research classes, choose one, sign up, attend the class, and practice the skills.

1. _____

2. _____

3. _____

4. _____

5. _____

Boundaries for children need to be easy to understand. It's tempting to make a rule for every possible situation, but this tends to be confusing for children and impossible for parents to enforce.

The most important boundaries for children of all ages are the ones that keep them physically and emotionally safe. To keep things simple, your remaining boundaries should reflect your values or what's most important to you, whether that's your children's education, manners, character, or health.

What safety-related boundaries will you prioritize with your children? Try to keep this list to three to six boundaries (fewer for younger kids, more for teenagers).

_____

_____

_____

_____

_____

What values-based boundaries will you prioritize with your children? Try to keep this list to two to three boundaries.

_____

_____

_____

_____

_____

If you have a partner, I encourage you to collaborate on identifying and prioritizing boundaries for your children.

Finally, let's address consequences: the actions you'll take when your children break the boundaries you set. Logical consequences 1) are directly related to the rule that was broken and 2) aim to teach children how to improve their behavior rather than shaming them or making them suffer.

To help you put logical consequences into practice, identify some common boundary issues for your children and some logical consequences. Be sure they meet the two criteria listed above.

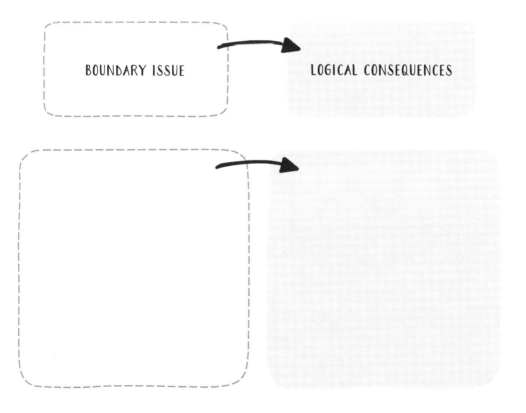

BOUNDARY ISSUE

LOGICAL CONSEQUENCES

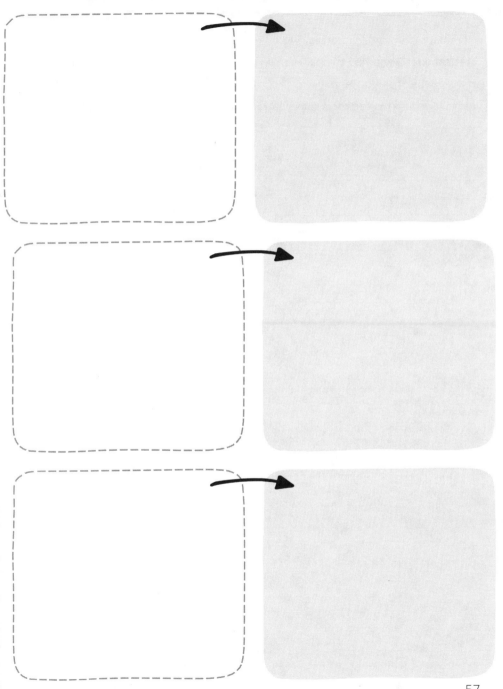

57

Eliminating boundary battles will take time and experimentation. To get started, identify a few things you can do to make a specific situation more manageable for you and your children. This might include changing the timing, who's involved, how expectations are communicated, and so forth.

Another way to be proactive about managing stress during boundary work—especially with your children—is to include regular self-care in your routine. Which of these self-care activities help you feel good?

- ○ Exercising
- ○ Eating regularly and in a reasonably healthy way
- ○ Getting enough sleep
- ○ Socializing and having fun
- ○ Having sex
- ○ Relaxing or having downtime
- ○ Utilizing medical care such as doctor's appointments
- ○ Doing creative activities
- ○ Identifying, accepting, and processing your feelings
- ○ Spending time alone
- ○ Other ideas: _____
- ○ _____
- ○ _____

Choose two self-care activities to prioritize. When and how will you make them more of a priority? **Example:** *I'll take a walk at lunchtime.*

_____

_____

_____

_____

Remember, self-care isn't all-or-nothing; every little bit helps, so don't create more stress by trying to do it all at once. Do what you can reasonably do and try to add a little bit more self-care over the coming weeks. Jot down some ideas that you can use when your children (or anyone you're setting boundaries with) are testing your patience.

_____

_____

_____

_____

_____

_____

_____

_____

Boundaries with Extended Family and Friends

Relationships with extended family members and friends come with expectations about how you'll interact, including how you parent, handle money, maintain privacy, divide your time, and celebrate holidays and special occasions.

Describe a boundary conflict that you've had with a family member or friend that you haven't been able to resolve.

_____

_____

_____

_____

What have you done to try to resolve this issue?

_____

_____

_____

_____

Even if you haven't been completely successful, give yourself a pat on the back for trying. Boundary issues with family and friends can be hard to solve because of the emotions and expectations involved. And knowing what doesn't work can also be valuable information that moves you closer to a solution.

Boundary norms vary greatly between families and cultures, and extended families and groups of friends are becoming increasingly diverse. Thinking about the boundary conflict you noted: what differences may be creating the conflict or misunderstandings about boundaries and expectations?

_____

_____

_____

_____

How do you think you've contributed to the conflict or misunderstanding? If you're not sure, are you willing to ask the other person?

_____

_____

_____

_____

_____

How can you get more information to help you understand the other person's beliefs, experiences, and needs?

How can you improve your communication skills to better understand and resolve your differences? Can you use I-statements, assertive language, acknowledgment of the other person's needs, and polite and specific requests rather than demands?

How can you show that you're receptive, accepting, and interested in learning and working together to solve the boundary conflict?

It can be painful to realize that we've been insensitive to someone's culture, made assumptions, or neglected to understand a different perspective. If this is the case for you, try to practice self-forgiveness because the alternative—feeling shame and guilt—doesn't help us build connections, learn, and compromise.

When I've made a mistake, I find relief by repeating this self-forgiveness mantra.

> *I forgive myself for my mistakes and shortcomings. I will not be self-critical and unkind to myself because that doesn't benefit anyone. Instead, I will put my energy into treating myself and others with love and respect. I'm committed to learning and growing so I can better understand others.*

You can use the space here to adapt this mantra or write your own.

_____

_____

_____

_____

_____

_____

Guilt also impedes our ability to set boundaries with family and friends. If this is true for you, let's dissect the experience to see what expectations or beliefs are creating those feelings.

Think of a boundary issue or person who tends to elicit feelings of guilt. What's expected of you in this situation or role (parent, child) that's contributing to these feelings?

_____

_____

_____

_____

_____

Use the space below to write down some of the strong beliefs or expectations your family might have of you. Then, consider: how strongly do they hold these beliefs? (Use a 1–10 scale.)

_____

_____

_____

_____

Notice the beliefs or expectations that you rated a five or higher. Choose one to practice with and write it in the space provided.

Example: I should drop everything when my mother needs something.

_____

_____

_____

Next, consider whether the belief or expectation is reasonable and makes sense to you.

Where did this belief or expectation come from? _____

_____

_____

Is this *your* belief or expectation or someone else's? _____

_____

_____

Is this belief or expectation helpful? _____

_____

_____

Does this belief or expectation allow you to care for yourself? _____

_____

Would you hold someone else to this same standard? _____

_____

_____

Are there exceptions to these absolutes (always, never)? _____

_____

_____

Who gets to decide what you have to or should do? _____

_____

_____

Does this expectation or belief align with your values? _____

_____

_____

Considering your answers, do you think the belief or expectation that you identified is realistic? Does it make sense to you? Why or why not?

_____

_____

_____

_____

_____

Rewrite the belief or expectation so it's more realistic and supportive of your needs.

_____

_____

_____

_____

When you feel confident about your beliefs and expectations, you won't be as susceptible to guilt. However, some of your family members and friends will probably still say that you're wrong or selfish because it's been an effective way to get what they want. To prepare for these challenges, write an affirmation or reminder that will help you cope and stay true to your new beliefs and expectations. You can use these prompts to help you.

I have a right to _____

I believe _____

It's okay that I can't please others all the time because _____

_____

Changing long-held beliefs and expectations takes quite a bit of practice and resolve. Keep practicing, and you'll gradually feel less guilty. This will make it easier for you to set the boundaries you need.

Enlisting the help of supportive people can also make setting boundaries with family and friends easier.

Sometimes, when we're setting boundaries, we need extra help. Take a few minutes now to practice enlisting help.

Identify a boundary issue that you're having with an extended family member or friend.

_____

_____

What kind of help do you need? Be specific.

_____

_____

_____

_____

Who's the best person to help you and why?

_____

_____

Asking for help can be a great tool when setting boundaries with anyone in your life—not just extended family members and friends.

For many couples, setting boundaries with extended family is a major source of conflict. It could be that your partner doesn't want to get involved, or they may actively undermine your efforts to set boundaries. In either case, it's painful to not have your partner's support.

Describe a boundary issue that you have with a family member for which you'd like your partner's support.

_____

_____

_____

_____

What do you need from your partner in this situation?

Example: _I need to feel loved and supported by my husband._

_____

_____

_____

Try using an I-statement to communicate your feelings and needs to your partner.

Example: _I feel_ hurt _when_ your mother insults me, _and I'd like_ you to ask her to stop and enforce consequences if she won't. _Is that something you're willing to help me with?_

I feel _____ when _____,

and I'd like _____.

Is that something you're willing to help me with?

If your partner agrees, you now have an opportunity to negotiate what the help will entail, when it will be given, and so forth.

When you have that conversation, come back to this journal to write about it. How did it go?

Boundaries with Difficult People

Sometimes, even when we do everything right, we still can't seem to set effective boundaries with certain people.

Is there someone in your life who consistently challenges your boundaries and disrespects you? If so, answer the following questions as you reflect on your experiences with them.

How does this person respond to your boundaries? Has their behavior made you reluctant to set boundaries?

What thoughts do you have when you interact with or anticipate interacting with this person?

How do you feel?

_____

_____

_____

_____

_____

How does your body respond?

_____

_____

_____

_____

_____

How else are you negatively affected by this person?

_____

_____

_____

_____

_____

When dealing with difficult people, we need to take a different approach to setting boundaries than we do with most people. We need to focus on being safe, avoiding power struggles, and knowing what we can control.

Although no one can definitively predict another person's behavior, past behavior is usually a strong indicator of future behavior. Describe this person's dangerous or harmful behaviors. Seeing these in writing can help you overcome any lingering denial. You can write this list somewhere more secure or make a mental note of the behaviors if you don't feel safe writing them here.

To make safety a priority for you (and your children, if you have any), consider proactive things you can do, such as the safety tips listed here:

- You do not need to explain or justify your boundaries to difficult people. Doing so can make matters worse. They will pick apart your reasons and use them to criticize and invalidate your needs. If communicating a boundary or consequence is likely to anger someone and put you in danger, you can take action to protect yourself without explanation. This might include leaving the situation, calling the police, or even moving out.

- If someone has been violent, aggressive, or threatening toward you or others, have potentially upsetting conversations in a public place or with another adult present.

- If you don't feel safe communicating in person, use text, email, or phone.

- If someone has been aggressive or threatening toward you or others, consider getting a restraining order.

- Create a safety plan that includes a safe place that you can go to, phone numbers of supportive people and community resources (such as shelters and crisis lines), cash, and identification.

What steps can you take to protect yourself from harm?

Since difficult people thrive on conflict, it falls on us to avoid power struggles.

How do difficult people pull you into power struggles or arguments? What do they say or do that consistently upsets you and causes you to react?

These are the behaviors that you need to be on the lookout for. The harder part, of course, is changing your response, so you don't get pulled into a power struggle.

What can you do instead of arguing, defending yourself, yelling, being sarcastic, or making demands? Try to list as many options as you can. If you have trouble with this, think about what someone else—a specific person you admire or an imaginary person who is wise, calm, and self-confident—would do.

> Since difficult people thrive on conflict, it falls on us to avoid power struggles.

We also need to be careful that we don't create power struggles by being controlling ourselves. How do you contribute to power struggles by forcing your agenda?

Difficult people don't want to change. When we accept this and stop trying to get them to change, we can focus on what we can control and get our needs met in another way.

Consider a situation from your own life. How is a difficult person violating one of your boundaries? For this exercise, think about one specific boundary violation.

_____

_____

_____

_____

_____

What personal needs are you trying to meet with this boundary?

_____

Assuming the difficult person behaves exactly as he or she has in the past, what can you do to get your needs met? Brainstorm as many options as possible regardless of whether they're "good" options.

_____

_____

_____

_____

_____

It's likely none of your options are ideal. Difficult people often leave us with few choices for setting and enforcing boundaries, which is why we may choose to accept imperfect solutions.

When you're wrestling with an imperfect solution, remember…

This boundary matters to me because: _____

_____

_____

I have the right to set boundaries because: _____

_____

_____

When a difficult person responds unfavorably, it doesn't mean I've done something wrong. It means: _____

_____

_____

I'm not responsible for how other people feel about my boundaries or how they respond.

I'm responsible for: _____

_____

In addition, when you're dealing with a difficult person or situation, I encourage you to increase your self-care—get enough sleep, exercise, spend time with supportive people, or enjoy a hobby. Difficult people can take a lot out of you, so it's important to replenish.

Boundaries help bring
relationships back
into balance.

PART 3

Set Better Boundaries

Four Steps to Better Boundaries

Step 1: Clarify Your Needs and Wants

Your boundaries are based on what you need and want in a particular situation. To clarify your needs and wants, ask yourself the following questions:

- What boundary-related problems am I experiencing?

- What are my unmet needs?

- How do I feel?

- What outcome do I want? What do I want to accomplish with my boundaries?

Understanding the problems that you're experiencing will give you important information about what you need and want. This will ultimately help you identify the boundaries that you need to set.

Describe one of your boundary-related problems. Try to be specific and stay focused on one problem or situation at a time.

Example: <u>Rachel is consistently late when we get together</u>.

Identify your unmet needs.

Example: <u>I need respect</u>.

_____

_____

_____

_____

Identify how you felt when you experienced the boundary-related problem.

Example: <u>Annoyed, disrespected, unimportant</u>.

_____

Incorporate the problems, needs, and feelings you've already identified into this formula to create your desired outcome statement. **Tip:** The way you want to feel is usually the opposite of how you feel when this problem occurs.

Example: _I need <u>respect</u> and want to feel <u>at ease, respected, and valued</u> when <u>I get together with Rachel</u>._

I need _____
(need)

and want to feel _____
(feeling)

when _____ .
(situation)

Your feelings can alert you to boundary problems and unmet needs.

Step 2: Identify Your Boundaries

Now that you know *what* you want to achieve, you can figure out *how* to create your desired outcome.

Identify five to ten ways to meet the unmet need(s) you identified in step one. Include *all* ideas, even if they don't seem viable.

1. _____

2. _____

3. _____

4. _____

5. _____

6. _____

7. _____

8. _____

9. _____

10. _____

When you're deciding what boundaries to set, you need to consider whether you can meet these needs yourself or whether you need to ask someone else to help you. You can ask others to change their behavior, but you can't control what they say, do, feel, or think. Fortunately, you can change your own thoughts, feelings, and actions—and doing so can often help you meet your needs.

Assuming nothing else changes, how can *you* meet your unmet needs? How can *you* create the feelings you want to have?

_____

_____

_____

_____

_____

_____

What behavior change can someone else make that will meet your unmet needs and help you create the feelings you want to have?

_____

_____

_____

_____

_____

Considering *all* the options that you've identified, which boundary makes the most sense for you to set? Remember, this is just a starting place; boundaries are flexible and can be changed.

_____

_____

Why did you choose this option?

_____

_____

_____

Once you've decided which boundaries will help you meet your needs and create positive feelings, you're ready to put them into action.

Step 3: Implement Your Boundaries

What will you do to set this boundary? Describe the actions that you'll take and the words that you'll use to communicate your boundary to others. Be as specific as possible.

_____

_____

_____

_____

_____

_____

When will you do this? Include date and time, if possible.

_____

_____

What action or change, if any, do you need to request from someone else?

_____

_____

_____

_____

When will you make this request?

_____

_____

What will you do if others resist, ignore, or respond with anger to your boundary? Again, be as specific as possible and include what, how, and when you'll say or do something.

_____

_____

_____

How will you know whether your boundary is effective?

_____

_____

_____

_____

What obstacles, if any, do you anticipate?

_____

_____

> **Boundaries are flexible and can be changed or adjusted.**

_____

_____

Who or what might help you get past these obstacles?

_____

_____

_____

_____

Step 4: Fine-Tune Your Boundaries

Boundaries are always a work in progress, and we rarely create just the right boundary on the first attempt. Use these questions to improve your boundaries and learn what worked and what adjustments you need to make.

What boundary did you try to set?

_____

_____

What worked about this boundary?

_____

_____

What didn't work about this boundary?

_____

_____

What needs were you trying to meet with this boundary?

_____

_____

Were your needs met? Rate how fully these needs were met.

0   1   2   3   4   5   6   7   8   9   10

What positive feelings did you hope to have as a result of creating this boundary?

_____

_____

Did your boundary help create positive feelings? Rate how strongly you felt the desired feelings. Remember, you aren't rating how you felt while setting the boundary, but how you felt in the same situation or with the same person after setting your boundary.

0   1   2   3   4   5   6   7   8   9   **10**

Overall, are you satisfied with this boundary? Did it meet enough of your needs and create enough of the feelings you hoped for?

_____

_____

_____

_____

_____

_____

_____

If yes, what is your plan for continuing to set this boundary? Be specific and include when and how you will do it.

_____

_____

_____

_____

_____

_____

_____

If no, the first question to ask yourself is whether you implemented your plan fully. And if not, you want to understand what got in your way, so you can figure out how to overcome this barrier.

What did you do to set your boundary?

_____

_____

_____

_____

_____

Which part of your plan didn't you follow through on?

_____

_____

_____

_____

_____

What got in your way? Was it fear or false beliefs about boundaries? Or was it a lack of planning or poor response from someone?

_____

_____

_____

_____

_____

You may also feel dissatisfied with the outcome if you misidentified your needs and feelings.

Do you have different or additional unmet needs that you didn't identify earlier?

_____

_____

_____

You will also need to adjust your boundary if you asked someone else to make a change, and they refused or didn't follow through with an agreed upon change. In this situation, you'll need to decide whether to ask again or meet this need yourself.

Was your request specific and clear? Did you communicate it respectfully and calmly? If not, how can you improve your request?

_____

_____

_____

_____

If you communicated your boundary clearly, and it wasn't respected, go back to your brainstorming list and see if you can create a new boundary plan that is within your control.

Is there a way for you to meet your needs yourself? How?

_____

_____

_____

Sometimes, we don't get the results we're looking for because we gave up too soon.

How many times have you tried to set this boundary?

_____

How long has this boundary issue been a problem? Usually, the longer the problem has existed, the longer it will take to change.

_____

Have you seen any improvement? Change isn't all-or-nothing, and in some situations, even a small improvement can be a sign that you're on the right track and should stay the course.

_____

_____

_____

_____

Do you think you've given this boundary enough time and effort to work? Why or why not?

_____

_____

_____

_____

How do you feel about continuing to set this boundary in the same way?

_____

_____

How do you feel about trying to set it differently?

_____

_____

After giving it some thought, does it make more sense to stick with your current plan or to make a different one?

_____

_____

Once you have a better idea of why your boundaries aren't as successful as you'd like, you can fine-tune your original boundary plan. Based on the pitfalls you identified, choose one or more of the adjustments listed below.

○ I will improve my follow-through by:

  ○ getting support or accountability from _____

  _____

  (specific people).

  ○ committing to do _____

  _____

  (specific action)

  on _____.

  (specific day/time)

  ○ other: _____

○ I will create a new boundary plan based on the additional needs
  I identified.

○ I will improve how I communicate my boundary by:

    ○ being more specific about what I need or want.

    ○ being polite and respectful.

    ○ making sure the other person hears and understands me.

    ○ staying calm.

    ○ using I-statements.

    ○ other: _____

○ I will create a new boundary plan based on things I can do rather than relying on someone else to change.

○ I will stick with my original plan and set this boundary at least _____ more times.

You should now have a list of actionable ways to adjust and improve your boundaries.

Manage Boundary Violations

Have you ever tried to set a boundary only to be ignored or not taken seriously? Perhaps you've had a friend or family member lash out in anger when you set a limit, or maybe they agreed to change their behavior but didn't follow through. If so, you aren't alone!

What kinds of boundary violations have you experienced?

_____

_____

_____

_____

_____

How does it feel when your boundaries are violated? How does it affect your relationship with the other person?

_____

_____

_____

_____

Think of a time when you weren't sure how to respond to a boundary violation or when your response didn't lead to the results you wanted. Describe the situation and some of the ways you could have responded.

_____

_____

_____

_____

_____

_____

Use the same situation to answer the following questions to get a better sense of the factors that influenced how you responded.

How important is it that this boundary is respected? Rate this on a scale of 1–10.

1   2   3   4   5   6   7   8   9   10

Then consider why you scored it as you did. Is it a deal-breaker when someone violates it? Is it a safety issue?

_____

_____

_____

_____

How were you affected by the boundary violation? How do you *feel* about it? Rate the strength of your feelings 1 to 10. (Higher levels of negative emotions such as anger, irritation, frustration, hopelessness, and sadness are another indication that this is an important boundary for you.) Then, write about it.

1   2   3   4   5   6   7   8   9   10

_____

_____

_____

_____

_____

_____

_____

_____

Understanding both how important the boundary is and how you were affected by the violation will help you figure out whether to respond and in what way. Note that safety issues always need to be addressed in some way, so recognizing that an issue is a safety concern signals that you need to do something to protect yourself or someone else.

Finally, consider how you acted in the situation you're writing about. How did you communicate your need or want? What did you say? What was your tone? Was your request clear and specific?

_____

_____

_____

_____

_____

_____

_____

_____

Were you heard? How do you know that you were understood?

_____

_____

_____

_____

_____

If your boundary was violated because you didn't make a specific request or weren't heard or understood, you might restate your boundary request before taking any other action.

What's the nature of your relationship with the person who violated your boundaries? How important is this relationship? Again, rate how important this relationship is from 1 to 10, then write about it.

1   2   3   4   5   6   7   8   9   **10**

_____

_____

_____

_____

_____

_____

Being aware of the nature and importance of the relationship will also help you decide how to respond.

Has this happened before? Is there a pattern of boundary violations by this person? If so, what does the pattern tell you?

_____

_____

_____

_____

If someone repeatedly disrespects your boundaries, it doesn't mean that you're "doing it wrong" or that you shouldn't set boundaries with this person. More likely, it means that you need to try a different approach to setting your boundary and increase your self-care to cope with this person.

Now you can decide whether you should respond to this boundary violation and if so, how.

Does this boundary violation warrant a response? Why or why not?

_____

_____

_____

_____

_____

_____

_____

When we respond to a boundary violation, it's usually by enforcing a consequence. A consequence is an action that you take in response to a boundary violation to protect yourself; its purpose isn't to punish others. It can be anything from leaving the room you're in to filing for divorce. When identifying a consequence, you might ask yourself, *How will this consequence help me protect and take care of myself?*

Using the same boundary violation that you identified in the previous exercise (or a different one, if you concluded no response was warranted), what consequences make sense and seem enforceable to you?

_____

_____

_____

_____

_____

_____

_____

_____

_____

_____

Now that you've identified some consequences, let's turn our focus to *how* to enforce them.

Depending on the situation, you may or may not want to explain the consequence to the other person. Sometimes, it's safer and easier to enact the consequence without explanation. If you're unsure whether to explain or state a consequence, consider the following aspects of the situation:

- whether it's safer to explain the consequence or not

- the nature and importance of the relationship

- the severity of the boundary violation or the intended consequence

- whether there's a pattern of boundary violations by this person that indicates they're unlikely to change

What are the pros and cons of verbally stating the consequence in the situation you've been writing about?

PROS

CONS

_____

_____

_____

_____

_____

Sometimes, boundary violations force us to make difficult choices. We can have a lot to lose—a relationship, job, or place to live—by enforcing the consequences of a boundary violation.

What boundary violation presents a difficult choice for you?

_____

_____

_____

_____

_____

How have you or others been hurt by this boundary violation?

_____

_____

_____

_____

_____

What keeps you from enforcing the consequences of this boundary violation? What might you lose if you enforce your boundaries?

_____

_____

_____

_____

_____

What might you gain?

_____

_____

_____

_____

_____

How do you feel when you think about what you've already lost versus what you might gain?

_____

_____

_____

_____

_____

_____

Give yourself permission to think about your options, feel your feelings, consult with trusted advisors (like close friends or counselors), or meditate or pray. You don't need to decide right now. But come back to these questions, continue to tune in to your thoughts, feelings, and needs, and value them— rather than avoiding or minimizing them. If you do this, you'll make the best decision for yourself in time.

Respect Other People's Boundaries

Everyone violates other people's boundaries from time to time. Often, these violations are minor infractions or accidents. But we all violate bigger boundaries too. So, I encourage you to take an honest look at your behavior because awareness is the first step to change.

> **Boundaries are a two-way street.**

Briefly describe one or two occasions when you've disrespected someone's boundaries.

_____

_____

_____

_____

_____

_____

In what ways have your relationships been negatively affected because you didn't respect other people's boundaries?

_____

_____

_____

_____

_____

_____

Try to view these incidences as learning opportunities; when you recognize your mistakes, you can learn to do better. Judging yourself harshly, on the other hand, is not productive.

Being told "no" is surprisingly difficult, regardless of how old or mature you are, because it can bring up a lot of difficult feelings and memories.

How do you feel when someone sets a limit that you don't like or tells you no?

_____

_____

_____

_____

How do you usually behave in such a situation?

_____

_____

_____

_____

You may notice that how you feel about other people's boundaries depends on who's setting the boundary, what the boundary is, and how the boundary is set.

Think of a boundary someone has set with you that's particularly painful. Does your reaction to this boundary seem justified? If not, can you think of how this boundary might be connected to a past experience?

Even if you can't figure out exactly where your intense feelings are coming from, it can be helpful to recognize that they're normal; they're your body's way of alerting you of a situation that was painful in the past. This allows you to notice what's different in this situation and look for signs that this person and their boundaries aren't a threat. When we don't perceive others as a threat, it's much easier to respect their boundaries.

> Respecting boundaries doesn't mean we necessarily agree with other peoples' decisions or opinions; it means we accept their right to make those decisions and have their opinions.

Asking for more information can help us avoid many boundary violations because we're more likely to overstep boundaries when we don't understand someone's needs or viewpoint.

Identify a situation in which you violated someone's boundaries. What clarifying questions would have helped you understand their boundaries and avoid disrespecting them?

_____

_____

_____

_____

_____

_____

In the future, how might you ask such questions in a way that they'll be well received? Consider your tone of voice, choice of words, timing, and so forth.

_____

_____

_____

_____

_____

_____

Perhaps the most important thing you can do to respect someone's boundaries is convey that you care and are interested in what they need. Here are some examples of phrases you can use to do this. Check off the ones you like and add your ideas.

- ○ I want to understand what you need.

- ○ I care about you and your needs.

- ○ Can we talk more about this?

- ○ I'm not always able to meet your needs or do what you want, but I do care about you.

- ○ Let's see if we can compromise.

- ○ We don't have to agree on everything to be friends.

- ○ I respect your opinion even though I disagree.

- ○ I don't want to overstep.

- ○ _____

- ○ _____

- ○ _____

You can also show care and consideration by being attentive and with a warm facial expression, gentle tone of voice, and relaxed body position.

Take Things Less Personally

When we take other people's boundaries personally, we perceive them as personal attacks or attempts to punish us when this may not be the case. The following exercise can help you identify the inaccurate thoughts that cause you to take things personally and replace them with thoughts that are more accurate and supportive. This can help you respect other people's boundaries.

Identify a boundary that someone's set with you that you're taking personally.

_____

_____

How do you feel about this boundary?

_____

_____

_____

Identify the specific thought, belief, or assumption that makes this boundary difficult for you to accept. **Example:** _I think Sam doesn't like being close to me._ Or: _I'm selfish._

_____

_____

_____

Next, look for and record evidence that supports or refutes the accuracy of this thought or belief.

_____

_____

_____

_____

_____

_____

_____

_____

_____

Finally, rewrite your thought or belief as a more accurate and supportive statement.

_____

_____

_____

Making Apologies and Improvements

When you violate someone's boundaries, it's important to apologize and change your behavior. Making a good apology, one that satisfies the person who was wronged, is more complicated than you might think. Researchers identified six components of an effective apology (Lewicki, Polin, and Lount 2016):

We're all human, and sometimes we make mistakes. When we violate other people's boundaries, it's important to apologize and change our behavior.

1. Acknowledge your responsibility.

2. Offer to repair the damage you've caused.

3. Express regret.

4. Explain what went wrong.

5. Make a declaration of repentance.

6. Request forgiveness.

With this in mind, practice writing an apology for a boundary you've disrespected.

_____

_____

_____

_____

_____

Apologies, even sincere ones, don't mean much if we continue to disrespect other people's boundaries. We also need to change our behavior.

What changes do you need to make to improve your ability to respect other people's boundaries? Be as specific as possible.

_____

_____

_____

_____

_____

_____

_____

How will you make these changes? What resources or help do you need?

_____

_____

_____

_____

_____

_____

_____

_____

Identifying what you need to change is a great start, and making a plan creates actionable steps to make the changes a reality.

Set Limits for Yourself

Most of us struggle to manage some aspects of our behavior, such as how much we spend, drink, or scroll on social media. Throughout this book, we've talked about how hard it is to say no to other people; it can be equally tough to say no to ourselves.

> To stay physically and emotionally healthy, reach our goals, and live according to our values, we need to set limits with ourselves.

Setting boundaries with yourself creates structure and predictability, which keep your life running smoothly, so you can be productive, stay healthy, and feel good about your choices.

How do you think setting limits with yourself can improve your life?

_____

_____

_____

_____

_____

There are three steps to setting boundaries with yourself: 1) identify areas of your life that need better self-management; 2) create goals to change your behavior; and 3) be kind to yourself when you make a mistake.

Take some time to reflect on what areas of your life need more structure or limits. What behaviors feel out of control or unpredictable, or create problems for you?

_____

_____

_____

_____

_____

Record the specific behaviors that you want to change, their negative effects, and how motivated you are to change them, using a 0–10 scale. You may want to do this over several days to give yourself time to identify a variety of self-management struggles.

The behavior:

The negative effects:

My motivation to change:　　0　1　2　3　4　5　6　7　8　9　10

The behavior:

The negative effects:

My motivation to change: 0   1   2   3   4   5   6   7   8   9   10

The behavior:

The negative effects:

My motivation to change: 0   1   2   3   4   5   6   7   8   9   10

The behavior:

The negative effects:

My motivation to change: 0 1 2 **3** **4** **5** **6** **7** **8** **9** **10**

People usually get the best results when they focus on one change or goal at a time. So, start with the behavior that's causing you the most problems and that you're highly motivated to change.

What behavior do you want to change first?

SMART goals are a simple and popular tool for setting goals; you may already be familiar with the concept. SMART is an acronym for specific, measurable, achievable, relevant, and time bound. Here's how we can apply this principle to self-management.

SMART GOAL

SPECIFIC. What specifically do you want to accomplish?

MEASURABLE. How will you know when you've achieved your goal? Measuring the outcome will tell you if you've accomplished what you set out to do.

ACHIEVABLE. Is your goal something that you can realistically accomplish? Is it within your control to achieve it? If not, adjust your goal so it's achievable. It's important to set yourself up for success by setting a modest goal.

RELEVANT. Does this goal align with your long-term goals and priorities? Does it seem worth doing? You want to spend your time and energy on goals that matter to you and are likely to improve your life.

TIME-BOUND. What is the timeline for accomplishing each step of your plan? A realistic schedule can help you make progress because you're more likely to follow through when you've specified when you'll do things.

Use this information to create a SMART goal for the behavior that you'd like to manage better.

BEHAVIOR TO CHANGE: _____

GOAL: _____

_____

_____

Setbacks are a natural part of the change process. Self-compassion can help you stick to your goals, even when things get hard.

Think of some occasions when you didn't manage your behavior as you wanted.

_____

_____

_____

_____

What did your inner critic say to you?

_____

_____

_____

_____

What were your fears?

How could you have responded with kindness and understanding, as you might respond to a friend in the same situation?

If your self-management struggles are causing significant problems or are getting worse, you may need more specialized or professional help. However, many of us don't seek help because we think it will be expensive, time-consuming, embarrassing, or hopeless.

What's preventing you from getting help?

_____

_____

_____

_____

_____

The barriers you're facing may be real—or they may be assumptions. So, do some research, ask friends, family members, and your doctor, call the 2-1-1 information line (available in most of the US), and talk to your health insurer and human resources department. There may be more options than you thought.

However, there may still be sacrifices involved in getting help—in which case you might think about what you could gain by getting help and what might happen if you don't.

What might you gain by seeking help?

_____

_____

_____

_____

_____

_____

What do you think will happen if you don't get help?

_____

_____

_____

_____

_____

_____

The bottom line is that seeking help and finding viable options takes perseverance and hard work, but it can ultimately help you take control of your life and rebuild your health and relationships.

Assertive communication
is essential to
setting boundaries.

PART 4

Practice Healthy

Communication

Ask for What You Need

Sometimes, a communication breakdown leads to a boundary not being followed. It's important to assertively ask for what you need. At first, it will feel awkward and take a lot of effort. But with practice, assertive communication gets easier and feels more natural, and you'll begin to see positive results in your relationships.

Using I-statements and being willing to compromise are two ways you can make more effective requests.

Here's the basic formula for an I-statement:

I feel _____ when/that _____

and I'd like _____.

To improve your I-statement, you can directly ask for the other person's agreement.

I would like you to _____.

Is that something you're willing to do?

If the other person agrees, you now have a clear agreement about what they will do differently. And if they don't agree, you can either work toward a compromise or, if that's not possible, take other actions to meet your needs and take care of yourself.

Practice completing the I-statement by repeating it, in writing and verbally.

_____

_____

_____

_____

_____

_____

_____

Not all requests are equally important, but when yours is, you should communicate it. Try practicing "It would mean a lot to me if..." statements.

It would mean a lot to me if _____

_____.

If the wording doesn't feel right to you, try these variations:

- _____ is really important to me.

- I would appreciate it if _____.

- I have a request that means a lot to me. It is _____.

- I'm very concerned about _____.

If you need a little bit more space to be creative, write your statements here:

_____

_____

_____

_____

_____

_____

If your boundary involves asking someone else to do something, it's helpful to remember that you're making a request, not a demand.

Think about accepting the reality that you can't *make* people do what you want—even when you set boundaries. How does that make you feel?

_____

_____

_____

In the end, this is one of those truths that can be hard to accept but can also be liberating: We can't make people do what we want. We *can* control what we do in response to what they do—the consequence that comes when a boundary we set is violated.

Be Specific

Another common communication problem is that we aren't clear about what we're asking for. You may have a general idea, such as, *I want to be treated with respect*, but you haven't identified what specifically you want the other person to do differently.

Here are some tips for making more specific requests:

- Whenever possible, identify an observable action that you want someone to make.

- Quantify how often, how much, or for how long you want the new behavior to last.

- Give specific times and dates.

- Give an example of what you're requesting.

See if you can rewrite the following boundary requests, so they're more specific.

I feel frustrated that you left a mess. I'd like you to help out more.

Please don't give my kids so much junk food.

Try writing a boundary request of your own, being as specific as possible.

Boundary Scripts

One of the most effective ways to practice setting boundaries is to write a script or an outline of what you want to say and how you'll say it. Following are some ideas to help you get started. However, we all need to find words that feel authentic and are appropriate for the situation at hand. So, use the space provided to tweak these phrases and add your own ideas.

Declining a Request or Invitation

- Unfortunately, I'm not available.

- I appreciate the invitation, but I need to decline.

- I don't think I'm the right person to help with that.

- I'm sorry, I can't help you this time.

- I'm overbooked and can't take on anything else.

- I have a personal policy of not going out on weeknights.

- _____

- _____

Setting Limits or Expectations

- I'll be back in ten minutes. I need a little time to myself.

- I need to leave promptly at four o'clock in the afternoon.

- I don't answer work emails on the weekend. I'll respond on Monday.

- I don't feel comfortable here. I'm going to go home.

- Dad, I don't have time to take you shopping this week. I'll place an order for you with the grocery delivery service.

- I know I told you that I'd help you move, but something has come up, and I won't be able to help.

- This is a deal-breaker for me. I can't compromise on behavior that's unsafe.

- _____

- _____

Making a Request

- We don't wear shoes in our house. Kindly take yours off when you come in.

- It would mean a lot if you could just listen and not offer solutions.

- Your comments about my appearance are hurtful, and I'd like you to stop.

- Please don't look through my phone without permission.

- That joke was insulting and not appropriate for the workplace. Please don't speak like that here.

- I don't want to talk about Zack when he's not here. Let's change the subject.

- Our wedding is for adults only. We'd love to see your children another time, but please don't bring them to this event.

- Johnny doesn't sleep well when he's had a lot of sugar; so please, no cookies.

- I'd like to connect with you. Can we agree to put our phones away while we eat?

- _____

- _____

Communicating When a Boundary is Crossed

- Your behavior is extremely hurtful. I'm going to spend the night at my brother's.

- Since you won't leave, I'm going to call the police.

- I'm going to hang up now.

- Infidelity is a deal-breaker for me, and I won't continue this relationship if you cheat on me.

- I've asked you multiple times to stop making sexualized comments about me, but you've continued. So, I've asked our boss to address it with you.

- I won't lend you money anymore. You didn't pay me back last time.

- _____

- _____

Try writing a script for a difficult boundary that you need to set. You can also include how you anticipate the other person will respond.

Once you've written your script, read through it a couple of times. Read it out loud. And then, make any necessary changes.

Manage Your Emotions

Setting boundaries can bring up a variety of challenging emotions. Before setting a boundary, it can help to take a brief time-out to notice how you're feeling. If you feel anxious, tense, or overwhelmed, try some of the following techniques.

Grounding is a quick and easy way to calm yourself. It *grounds* you in the present, so you aren't ruminating about the past or worrying about the future.

To begin, rate your stress or anxiety on a scale of 1–10:

1   2   3   4   5   6   7   8   9   10

Take a few slow, deep breaths. Then, ask yourself the following questions.

Name 5 things you can see: _____

_____

_____

How many electrical outlets are in the room you're in? _____

What does the chair or couch you're sitting on feel like? Is it soft? Rough? Smooth? _____

_____

How many green items can you see? _____

What do you smell? _____

_____

Describe the shoes you're wearing in as much detail as possible: _____

_____

_____

_____

_____

_____

_____

Name three sounds you hear: _____

_____

Pick up a nearby object. What does it feel like? How much does it weigh?

_____

_____

Rerate your anxiety on a scale of 1–10:

1   2   3   4   5   6   7   8   9   10

If the score is greater than 5, repeat the grounding exercise.

In the future, you can do this exercise mentally, without writing down your answers.

You can also try using a *mantra*. A mantra is a positive statement that you repeat to yourself to help motivate, encourage, or calm yourself. Read the examples below and try writing your own.

1. *I've got this.*

2. *I'm calm and confident.*

3. *I can handle whatever happens.*

4. *It's okay to ask for what I need.*

Here are some other ways to self-soothe when you need to:

- Go for a walk.

- Take a bath or shower.

- Write down your thoughts and feelings.

- Listen to calming music.

- Stretch.

- Rub your shoulders and neck.

- Inhale for a count of four, hold your breath for a count of four, exhale for a count of four, hold for a count of four; repeat for one to two minutes. This is called box breathing.

- Place your hand over your heart, notice your chest rising and falling with each breath. Expand your chest as much as you can with each inhale. As you exhale, visualize tension flowing out like air leaving a deflating balloon.

- Think of ten things you're grateful for.

- Pet your cat or dog.

Use the space below to note the strategies that you're open to trying, as well as any other self-soothing strategies that work well for you.

- _____
- _____
- _____
- _____
- _____
- _____
- _____
- _____
- _____
- _____
- _____
- _____
- _____
- _____
- _____

Compromise (When It Makes Sense)

As we discussed earlier, boundaries sometimes involve compromise, which is usually good for both parties. However, be careful about being too accommodating. Many people who struggle with boundaries confuse compromising and conceding. Conceding is one party giving in, whereas compromising involves a give-and-take between both parties.

Take a moment to list how you've felt in the past when you know you've conceded, as well as how the other person treated you and how your body reacted.

We all have some nonnegotiable boundaries—things we aren't willing to compromise on—and that's okay. Just make sure that you don't categorize too many boundaries as deal-breakers because then you're probably becoming too rigid with your boundaries or making idle threats. Aim to identify just four to five nonnegotiable boundaries that you need in your life right now.

What are your nonnegotiable boundaries?

1. _____

2. _____

3. _____

4. _____

5. _____

Now that you know what your nonnegotiable boundaries are, you can try to be flexible and open to compromise on your other boundaries.

If achieving true compromise in your relationships is difficult, here are some additional questions and statements that you can use to promote compromise.

- How can we work together to get both of our needs met?

- I'd like to find a solution that will work for both of us.

- If we're both willing to give a bit, I'm sure we can reach an agreement.

- I think we have the same goal. We just need to hammer out the details.

- What would work for you?

- I need _____ from you. What do you need from me?

- Can we try it this way, and then if it doesn't work for you, we'll renegotiate?

- I'd like to hear what you think.

- I need _____, but I'm open to hearing your ideas about how I can get/do this in a way that will work for you too.

Using new communication skills can be challenging. The most important thing is that you keep working at them. Your skills will improve the more you use them!

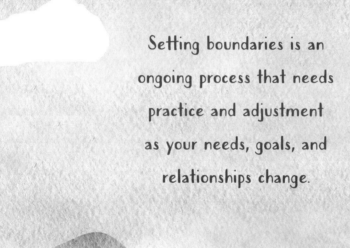

Setting boundaries is an
ongoing process that needs
practice and adjustment
as your needs, goals, and
relationships change.

PART 5

Keep Learning

As you know, setting boundaries is hard work. You may feel discouraged or unmotivated sometimes, especially when you make mistakes and encounter setbacks. The following tips can help you stay motivated and continue to learn.

Learn from Mistakes

It doesn't feel good to make mistakes, so we usually try to avoid them. But mistakes are a normal part of the learning process—and they can even be helpful. Try to reframe one of your recent boundary-setting mistakes as a learning opportunity. The following questions can help.

Identify a boundary-setting mistake.

_____

_____

_____

What did you learn from this experience?

_____

_____

_____

_____

_____

_____

What will you do differently next time?

_____

_____

_____

_____

What skills do you need to practice further?

_____

_____

_____

What went well in this attempt to set a boundary?

_____

_____

_____

_____

_____

Be Kind to Yourself

We need to watch that frustration and disappointment don't lead to self-criticism. This is demotivating and makes it harder to set boundaries because it reinforces negative beliefs about ourselves. Offering yourself kindness is more productive and will lead to better results in the future. One way to do this is by saying something compassionate and reassuring to yourself, such as:

- This is hard, but I'll try again.

- I'll succeed if I keep at it.

- Everyone makes mistakes and does things imperfectly.

- The more I practice, the easier this will get.

- I'm choosing to confront my fears.

- It's normal to feel uncomfortable and afraid when setting new boundaries.

- Uncomfortable feelings will pass.

- I have the right to be treated with dignity and respect.

If you feel discouraged, what compassionate words can you offer yourself?

Notice Your Successes

Another way to stay motivated and build confidence is to intentionally draw attention to your successes and progress.

List some of your boundary-setting successes. Remember, you're looking for progress, not perfection.

Keep applying your skills and reflecting on what you've been doing and learning, and you'll find your boundaries, relationships, and life continue to improve.

Reference

Lewicki, R. J., B. Polin, and R. B. Lount, Jr. 2016. "An Exploration of the Structure of Effective Apologies." *Negotiation and Conflict Management Research* 9: 177–196.

Real change *is* possible

For more than forty-five years, New Harbinger has published proven-effective self-help books and pioneering workbooks to help readers of all ages and backgrounds improve mental health and well-being, and achieve lasting personal growth. In addition, our spirituality books offer profound guidance for deepening awareness and cultivating healing, self-discovery, and fulfillment.

Founded by psychologist Matthew McKay and Patrick Fanning, New Harbinger is proud to be an independent, employee-owned company. Our books reflect our core values of integrity, innovation, commitment, sustainability, compassion, and trust. Written by leaders in the field and recommended by therapists worldwide, New Harbinger books are practical, accessible, and provide real tools for real change.

 **newharbinger**publications

SHARON MARTIN, DSW, LCSW, is a licensed psychotherapist and mental health writer specializing in codependency, perfectionism, and healthy relationships, with a private practice in San Jose, CA. She is author of *The CBT Workbook for Perfectionism* and *The Better Boundaries Workbook*.

Also by Sharon Martin

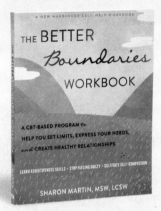

This evidence-based workbook will show you how to set healthy
boundaries across all aspects of life—without sacrificing your
kindness or compassion for others.

ISBN 978-1684037582 / US $24.95

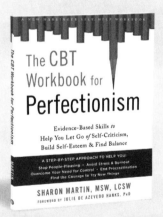

If you're ready to break free from perfectionism and start living a
richer, fuller life, this workbook will help you get started.

ISBN 978-1684031535 / US $24.95

newharbingerpublications
1-800-748-6273 / newharbinger.com